EXPLORE THE U.S.A.

NORTH CAROLINA

Cindy Rodriguez

www.av2books.com

LET'S READ
AV²
BY WEIGL™
ADDED VALUE • AUDIO VISUAL

Go to **www.av2books.com**, and enter this book's unique code.

BOOK CODE

Z220797

AV² by Weigl brings you media enhanced books that support active learning.

AV² provides enriched content that supplements and complements this book. Weigl's AV² books strive to create inspired learning and engage young minds in a total learning experience.

Your AV² Media Enhanced books come alive with...

Audio
Listen to sections of the book read aloud.

Video
Watch informative video clips.

Embedded Weblinks
Gain additional information for research.

Try This!
Complete activities and hands-on experiments.

Key Words
Study vocabulary, and complete a matching word activity.

Quizzes
Test your knowledge.

Slide Show
View images and captions, and prepare a presentation.

... and much, much more!

Published by AV² by Weigl
350 5th Avenue, 59th Floor
New York, NY 10118
Website: www.av2books.com   www.weigl.com

Library of Congress Cataloging-in-Publication Data
Rodriguez, Cindy.
  North Carolina / Cindy Rodriguez.
    p. cm. -- (Explore the U.S.A.)
Includes bibliographical references and index.
ISBN 978-1-61913-385-3 (hard cover : alk. paper)
1. North Carolina--Juvenile literature. I. Title.
F254.3.R63 2013
975.6--dc23
                          2012015609

Printed in the United States of America in North Mankato, Minnesota
1 2 3 4 5 6 7 8 9 16 15 14 13 12

052012
WEP040512

Project Coordinator: Karen Durrie
Art Director: Terry Paulhus

Weigl acknowledges Getty Images as the primary image supplier for this title.

NORTH CAROLINA

Contents

This is North Carolina.
It is called the Tar Heel State.
Tar was important to the state
many years ago.

This is the shape of North Carolina. It is in the east part of the United States. North Carolina borders four other states.

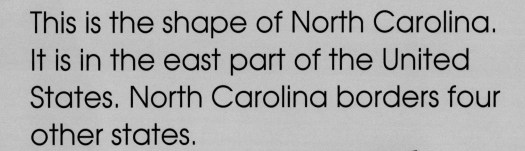

Where is North Carolina?

Canada

United States

Pacific Ocean

Atlantic Ocean

Mexico

North Carolina is next to the Atlantic Ocean.

The first airplane flight took place in North Carolina in 1903. Orville and Wilbur Wright flew the airplane in the town of Kitty Hawk.

The first airplane flew for 12 seconds and covered 120 feet.

The dogwood is the North Carolina state flower. This flower grows on trees that can be up to 30 feet tall.

The North Carolina state seal has two women, a ship, and mountains.

The two women are the goddesses of Liberty and Plenty.

This is the state flag of North Carolina. It is red, white, blue, and yellow.

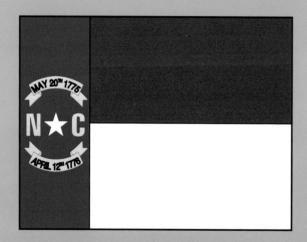

The North Carolina flag has one white star.

The gray squirrel is the state animal of North Carolina. This animal lives in all parts of the state.

Squirrels have four teeth that never stop growing.

Raleigh is the capital city of North Carolina. It was one of the first cities built by British settlers in the United States.

Raleigh is called the City of Oaks for its many oak trees.

1795 1849
JAMES KNOX POLK
OF
MECKLENBURG COUNTY

PRESIDENT
1845 - 1849

HE ENLARGED OUR
NATIONAL BOUNDARIES

1767 1845
ANDREW JACKSON
OF
UNION COUNTY

PRESIDENT
1829 - 1837

HE REVITALIZED
AMERICAN DEMOCRACY

1808 1875
ANDREW JOHNSON
OF
WAKE COUNTY

PRESIDENT
1865 - 1869

HE DEFENDED
THE CONSTITUTION

NO CLIMBING
ON STATUES

Sweet potatoes grow in North Carolina. The state grows more sweet potatoes than California, Louisiana, and Mississippi together.

North Carolina is also known for the furniture made there.

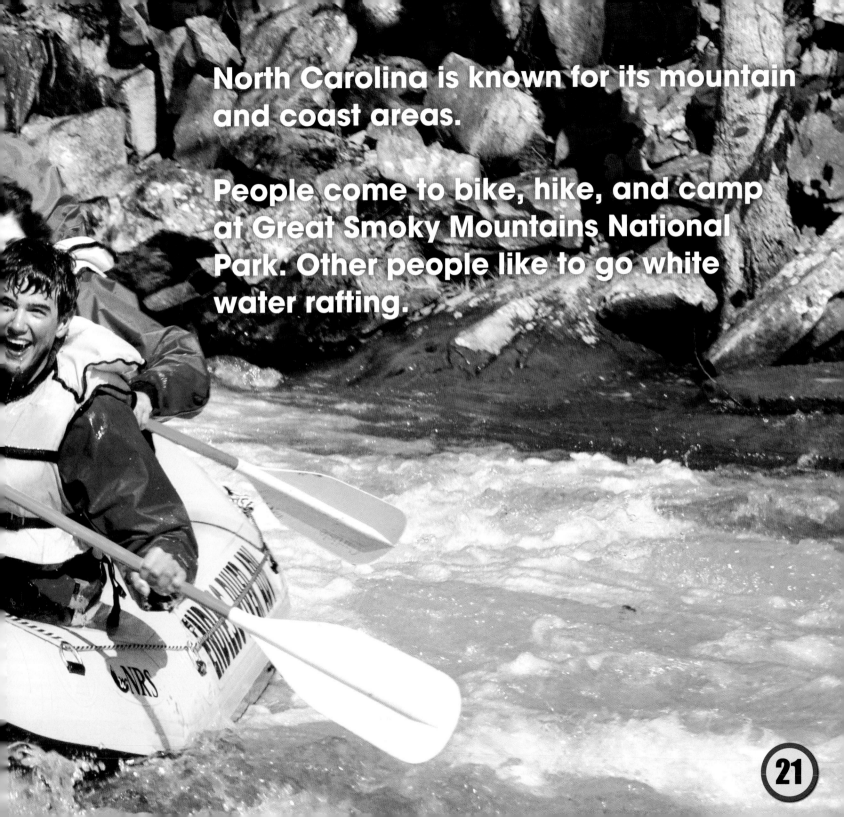

North Carolina is known for its mountain and coast areas.

People come to bike, hike, and camp at Great Smoky Mountains National Park. Other people like to go white water rafting.

21

NORTH CAROLINA FACTS

These pages provide detailed information that expands on the interesting facts found in the book. These pages are intended to be used by adults as a learning support to help young readers round out their knowledge of each state in the *Explore the U.S.A.* series.

Pages 4–5

The Tar Heel State nickname may refer to the tar early settlers extracted from the pine forests in the area. Before the American Revolution, North Carolina exported more than 100,000 barrels of tar and pitch each year. The tar and pitch was used to seal the wooden hulls of ships in order to keep water out.

Pages 6–7

On November 21, 1789, North Carolina joined the United States as the 12th state. North Carolina's neighbors are Virginia to the north and Tennessee to the west. South Carolina and Georgia share North Carolina's southern border. The Atlantic Ocean lies to the east. Along the shoreline is the Outer Banks, a small chain of islands that have many lighthouses. Cape Hatteras, the state's easternmost point, has been the site of numerous shipwrecks.

Pages 8–9

Orville and Wilbur Wright chose Kitty Hawk, North Carolina, for their flight tests because of its high winds and tall dunes. They launched from the dunes and used the wind to help keep the airplane in the air. On December 17, 1903, Orville made the first successful powered flight. Later that day, Wilbur flew the plane 852 feet (259 meters) in 59 seconds.

Pages 10–11

Dogwood blossoms appear in spring and summer. They are mostly white but can also be light pink or red. North Carolina's seal has changed many times over the years. The current seal shows two women. They are Liberty, representing North Carolina's independence from England, and Plenty with her cornucopia, depicting the state's abundance of food. The ship and mountains symbolize the state's varied landscapes.

North Carolina's flag has three bars of color. The blue vertical bar stands for the Union. It includes a white star and the state's initials in yellow. The star symbolizes North Carolina's position as one of the first 13 states to join the United States. The yellow banners also show the two dates declaring North Carolina's independence from Great Britain.

The gray squirrel is found across North Carolina, from its eastern swamps to its western hardwood forests. It is part of the rodent family and spends most of its life in trees. Gray squirrels live in tree cavities, such as woodpecker holes, or in nests made from dead leaves. Squirrels must constantly chew on things to keep their teeth from growing too long.

Raleigh is the largest city in what is known as the Research Triangle. This 7,000-acre (2,800-hectare) area contains offices and laboratories for more than 170 companies. Settlers called Raleigh the City of Oaks. They tried to keep the city's many forests and parks healthy. The city is named for Sir Walter Raleigh, who founded the first English colony in the area in 1584.

Two-fifths of all U.S. sweet potatoes come from North Carolina. This is more than the next three leading sweet potato growing states combined. In 2010, North Carolina harvested more than 50,000 acres (20,200 hectares) of sweet potatoes. The state is also known for making furniture. The city of High Point is known as the Furniture Capital of the World. The High Point Market is the world's largest furniture trade fair.

White water rafting is an activity enjoyed by visitors to the mountains of western North Carolina. Grandfather Mountain has the nation's highest swinging bridge, measuring 1 mile (1.6 kilometers) high. Tourists also like to see the beautiful lighthouses on the Outer Banks Islands. Cape Hatteras is home to the tallest lighthouse in the United States.

KEY WORDS

Research has shown that as much as 65 percent of all written material published in English is made up of 300 words. These 300 words cannot be taught using pictures or learned by sounding them out. They must be recognized by sight. This book contains 59 common sight words to help young readers improve their reading fluency and comprehension. This book also teaches young readers several important content words, such as proper nouns. These words are paired with pictures to aid in learning and improve understanding.

Page	Sight Words First Appearance
4	important, is, it, many, state, the, this, to, was, years
7	four, in, next, of, other, part, where
8	and, feet, first, for, place, seconds, took
11	a, are, be, can, grows, has, mountains, on, that, trees, two, up
12	one, white
15	all, animal, have, lives, never, stop
16	by, city, its
19	also, made, more, than, there, together
21	at, come, go, like, people, water

Page	Content Words First Appearance
4	heel, North Carolina, tar
7	Atlantic Ocean, shape, United States
8	airplane, flight, Kitty Hawk, Orville, Wilbur Wright, town
11	dogwood, flower, goddesses, Liberty, Plenty, seal, ship, women
12	flag, star
15	gray squirrel, teeth
16	Raleigh, settlers
19	California, furniture, Louisiana, Mississippi, sweet potatoes
21	areas, Great Smoky Mountains National Park, rafting

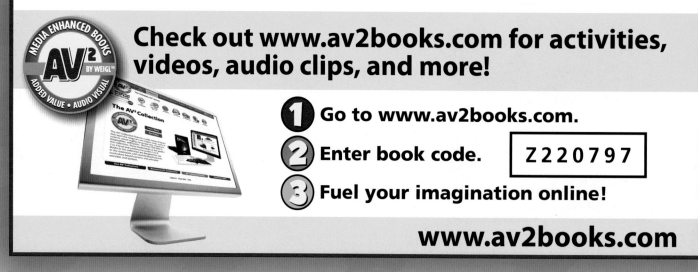